KU-616-351

RAYMOND BRIGGS

Ethel & Ernest

JONATHAN CAPE
London

For my Mother & Father

This edition published 1999

2 4 6 8 10 9 7 5 3 1

© 1998 Raymond Briggs

Raymond Briggs has asserted his right under the Copyright, Designs
and Patents Act 1988 to be identified as the author of this work

First published in Great Britain in 1998 by Jonathan Cape
Random House, 20 Vauxhall Bridge Road, London SW1V 2SA

Random House Australia (Pty) Limited
20 Alfred Street, Milsons Point, Sydney,
New South Wales 2061, Australia

Random House New Zealand Limited
18 Poland Road, Glenfield,
Auckland 10, New Zealand

Random House South Africa (Pty) Limited
Endulini, 5A Jubilee Road,
Parktown 2193, South Africa

Random House UK Limited Reg. No. 954009
A CIP catalogue record for this book
is available from the British Library

ISBN 0 224 06039 2

Printed and bound in Singapore
by Tien Wah Press (Pte) Ltd

Ethel & Ernest

TUESDAY

WEDNESDAY

THURSDAY

FRIDAY

SATURDAY

5

Victor Mc Laglen!

Who's he?

Him up there.

Oh.

My favourite!

Oh.

Lovely flowers, darling.

Oh, that's Dad. He's potty about the garden.

Did you all grow up here?

Yes. Eleven of us. Thirteen with Mum and Dad. Bob, Beaty, Mag, Edie, me, Frank, Flo, Jessie, George, Joe and Bill.

George was killed in the war. Bob died as a baby. Beaty died at two and a half.

1930
~
1940

10

11

ENORMOUS bedroom!

FOUR windows in one room!

It'll cost a fortune for curtains...

THREE bedrooms for TWO people! Bit different to home, eh, darling?

Perhaps there'll be more than two, one day...

What? Lodgers, you mean?

NO!

This could be our BABY's room!

Nice and warm over the kitchen.

Good little shed for my bike and workshop.

Mind you keep it tidy!

Now don't you start bossing me about BEFORE we're married!

13

The Lovers' Seat

Fairlight Glen · Hastings · 1930

16

17

I've finished the tiling. It's got a back boiler and that's the hot tank up there, see?

Ugly.

I'll box it in with tongue and groove, dear.

Then paint it a nice pastel shade.

Cor! Over **TWO MILLION** unemployed!

I'm lucky to be a milkman.

Doesn't it look lovely?

Very posh.

Four chairs and two carvers, Ernest! Almost new!

Jacobean!

Whatever are you up to now?

Cement mixing. Making a bird bath.

19

23

24

This gas copper is a real luxury!

Just turn the tap and strike a match!

The BBC's going to start "Tele-vision" later this year...

Oh? What's that when it's at home?

Well, it looks like a wireless set with pictures on top of it.

MOVING pictures? Talkies?

Yes. It'll be like going to the pictures without going out.

What? You'll just sit and look at it?

Yes.

I suppose it might be all right for the gentry.

26

29

Whatever are you home for?
You're supposed to be AT SCHOOL!
You mustn't come home in the MIDDLE OF THE DAY!
Did you cross that main road you must have done!

I can't find the
sit down lavatories.
We SHOWED you them!
No. They're GIRLS.
Girls sit down.
NO! There's BOYS' sitting downs as well.

No there ISN'T!
It's all GIRLS.
Look out!
I want to go Number Twos.

Sounds like that Hitler's on the warpath good and proper.

Our George was killed in the last one.

And brother Tom.

It doesn't seem all that long ago.

Our poor old mother never got over it. She died at 4

Mum!
What have I got to wear
red, white and blue
to school for?
Because it's Empire Day.
What's empire?

Do keep STILL!

Hitler's marched into Prague, now.

He'll be coming down our road soon.

Adolf Hitler in Wimbledon Park!

It's going to be very stuffy with all this blackout up, Ernest.

Not half as stuffy as a gas-proof room would be.
You have to bung up the chimney, tape over the cracks round doors and windows, put wet newspapers in between the floorboards...

It's a right old barney.

POISON GAS!

I hadn't thought of that.

♩ Underneath the spreading chestnut tree, Mr. Chamberlain said to me, ♪ if you want your gas mask fitted free — Join the blinking A.R.P. ♩

34

Mind my antirrhinums, Ernest.

I hope you know what you're doing.

Is that it finished?

That's it. All done!

Is it really bombproof?

We'll have to wait and see.

36

Russia's invaded Finland now.   I thought they'd invaded POLAND?

Yes, they have.   But you said GERMANY's invaded Poland?

Yes, that's right.   Well, who was it invaded Czechoslovakia?

Germany.   Germany's always invading someone.
I expect they'll invade Russia one day –

Cor blimey! Not likely!
They're IN LEAGUE!   or Russia will invade Germany.

Oh don't be DAFT!   If they ALL keep invading one another,
WE'LL end up invading someone.

Oh Et! You just don't
understand politics.

1940
~
1950

The battle for France is over...
the Battle of Britain is about to begin.
Upon this battle depends the survival
of Christian civilization.
The whole fury and might of the enemy
must, very soon, be turned on us.
Hitler knows that he will have to break us
in this island, or lose the war.

If we can stand up to him, all Europe
may be free and the life of the world
may move forward into broad sunlit uplands.

But, if we fail, the whole world
will sink into the abyss of a new dark age.
Let us, therefore, brace ourselves to our duty
and so bear ourselves that if the
British Empire last for a thousand years,
men will still say:

THIS was their finest hour.

Broad sunlit uplands!

Good old Winston!
Our finest hour!

I expect Jerry will be coming over soon.

They're starting to take away our nice gate and railings.

I'll make a wooden gate.

Shame.

They want saucepans, too. They make them into Spitfires.

Funny to think of our front gate being a Spitfire.

46

47

49

Here!
The Court of Appeal
has ruled that savings
from housekeeping money
BELONG TO THE HUSBAND.

YOU don't save from
the housekeeping money,
do you, dear?

No, never.
Only to buy your
birthday present.

See? Told you.
We've signed a pact
with old Joe Stalin.
"TWENTY YEAR PACT
THROUGH WAR AND PEACE."

It's TWENTY YEARS!

Er... well...
I dunno...

Cor! Look!
"Women's Fashions—"
"SHORTER SKIRTS—"
"Bare legs for Patriotism,"
it says—

Very nice.
As long as it lasts.

And how many years
was his pact with Hitler?

ERNEST!

Dearest!
I've been PROMOTED!
I am now a CLERK!
CLERK GRADE B3!

No more packing
parcels in that rotten,
freezing warehouse?

NO! I'm going to
work in an
OFFICE!

51

Look! It's come up!

What's that, son?

A pear tree! Auntie Flo gave me the pips from a pear we ate.

It had better not get too big, it'll block out all the light.

Don't discourage the boy, Ernest, I like a nice pear.

DARLING! **LABOUR'S WON!** WE'RE IN!

LABOUR WINS

Such a shame for poor Mr. Churchill.

The working man will be all right now. AT LAST!

He saved our bacon in the war.

Bloody MARVELLOUS!

ERNEST! Mr. Churchill never swears. He's a gentleman.

I'm Labour, Mum.

Sssh, dear.

58

60

1950
~
1960

Dad... Hullo.

Dad...
When you come
home from work... Yeah?
Why don't you wash
in the BATHROOM? Blimey son! Not likely! I'm filthy, look.

Yes, I know but that is
what the bathroom is FOR! No. Not in the BATHROOM.
Not in THIS state.

But this is the KITCHEN!
All the FOOD is in HERE!
Mum is trying to COOK! No. I couldn't, son.
Not in the BATHROOM.

That laundrette is a Godsend!
I did the whole blessed lot
for two and nine.
AND it's all bone DRY!

We could chuck out the mangle and the copper.
I could get an electric thermostat for the tank!
Hot water in the SUMMER time!
MODERN!

71

72

73

Dear, oh dear...
"BRITISH RAIL LOSES
SIXTEEN MILLION QUID"

It's Nationalised,
isn't it?

'COURSE
IT IS!

I thought so.

It says they're wanting to
legalise Homo-sexuality.   Oh? What's that?

Well...you know...it's like-
two BLOKES.
Only... instead of with a WOMAN,
sort of with-one another...like...

I don't know what
you're rambling on
about, Ernest, and I don't
think you do either.

I'll... er-put the kettle on,
shall I, duck?
Nice cup of tea?

75

Here Et, listen. It says we've got to be **HIP.**

What?

GROOVY, babe. And **REAL COOL.**

Just talk sense, Ernest.

We've got to **HANG LOOSE** with the **CATS.**

Cats?

YEAH, MAN!

Ernest! Go to bed.
You're overtired.
I'll make the cocoa.

You're a **SQUARE,** baby.

Oh, Ernest...
When will you grow up?

1960
~
1970

That green car! / Well?
Triumph Herald! / What about it?
Wasn't there yesterday. / There's always different cars stuck outside our house nowadays.

That one's special. / What's special about it?

It's OURS!

Oh don't be daft, Ernest.

Come on, dear. Get in. / Ooh-er... I don't like to... I've still got my pinny on.

I haven't done my hair.

Is it really yours?

OURS, darling.

I didn't know you could drive a proper car.

81

83

OH, NO! He says they're going to get married in a **REGISTRY OFFICE!**

Well, that's the modern way, Et.

Horrible!

Yes, but neither of them is religious.

I don't want him to be **RELIGIOUS!**

It's so much... nicer...

I just want him to get married in a **CHURCH!**

When are you going to start a family, dear?

Well... don't know really, Mum. Probably not at all.

Goodness me! Why ever not? I want to be a granny.

Well, Jean's got problems, Mum. Brain trouble.

BRAIN TROUBLE!

Yeah...well...that's just what I call it - as a sort of...joke...

She goes in and out of the loony bin.

You mean...she's - mental?

Yeah. That's one word for it. The other word is - Schizophrenia.

Oh, dear! Poor thing!

So I won't be a granny after all?

Never mind, Mum.

87

MAN ON THE MOON, Et!

FANTASTIC, eh? *Oh?*

What's he doing there?

Well, just walking about a bit.

Then what?

Well...come back, I suppose...

Perhaps they'll have a picnic.
That would be nice.

I think the tea would blow away
when it came out of the thermos.

Why? Is it windy up there?

No, it's gravity, dear.

Oh, I see.

Look! He's going to pick up
some pebbles...to take home.

Just like kiddies at the seaside.
Turn it off, will you?

1970
~
1971

Decimal Currency starts next week!   Oh yes, I've heard about it on the television.

It's dead simple! See - a bob equals **FIVE** New Pence. Two bob is **TEN** New Pence.   What's a ha'penny?

There isn't one - oh yes, there is! Half a New Pence - looks like a farthing.   What about threepenny bits?

Gone, duck. A tanner is two and a half New Pence.   And what about half a crown?

Er...well...that'll be - two bob equals ten New Pence, a tanner equals two and a half New Pence, so ten plus two and a half is...twelve and a half New Pence. Easy!   What's a penny?

An **OLD** penny...well...a shilling is five New Pence, so twelve old pennies equals five **NEW** Pence, so **ONE** old penny is...twelve into five - Um...   How many shillings are there in the pound now?

90

92

Leabharlann Átha Cliath Theas

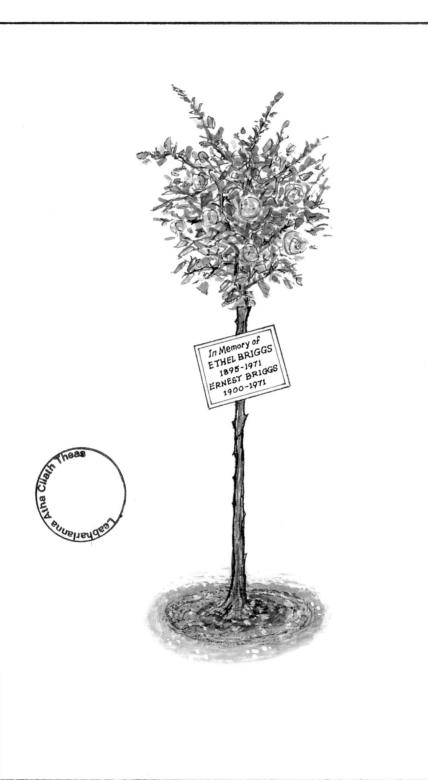

In Memory of
ETHEL BRIGGS
1895-1971
ERNEST BRIGGS
1900-1971

Leabharlanna Atha Cliath Theas